Poems of Inspiration and Comfort

Poems of
Inspiration
and Comfort

Edited by Gail Harvey

GRAMERCY BOOKS
New York • Avenel

Compilation and introduction
Copyright © 1990 by Outlet Book Company, Inc.
All rights reserved
Published by Gramercy Books,
distributed by Outlet Book Company, Inc.,
a Random House Company,
40 Engelhard Avenue,
Avenel, New Jersey 07001.

Manufactured in Malaysia

Designed by Melissa Ring

Library of Congress Cataloging-in-Publication Data
Poems of inspiration and comfort.
        p.   cm.
    ISBN 0-517-03152-3
    1. Inspiration—Poetry.   2. English poetry.
3. American poetry.
PR1195.I55P64   1990
821.008'0353—dc20   90-31412
                                            CIP

        14   13   12   11   10   9   8   7

Contents

Introduction

"*Poetry* expresses the universal," wrote Aristotle, and, indeed, only poetry can express the complex depths of human emotion, the ephemeral qualities of love, the nostalgia for days long past, the agony of loss, the whirlpools of despair, the mysteries of death. Poetry also can enter the soul. It can inspire hope and aspirations and evoke beauty and delight. In the dark coldness of winter it can remind us that the gentle warmth and golden days of spring lie just ahead. Truly, poetry does have the power to heal.

Poems of Inspiration and Comfort is a new collection of memorable poetry written by some of the world's greatest poets. Emily Dickinson, for example, writes of hope "that perches in the soul, And sings the tune without the words, And never stops at all." William Cowper reminds us that God moves in a mysterious way, and John Milton inspires us with his moving poem about his blindness. James Russell Lowell exuberantly describes a day in June and Oliver Wendell Holmes writes with wit and wisdom about growing old. William Cullen Bryant serenely contemplates the inevitability of death in *Thanatopsis*, one of his most famous poems, written when he was only sixteen years old. Walt Whitman extols the world's miracles and Henry Wadsworth Longfellow reminds us that "We can make our lives sublime . . ." and "leave behind us, Footprints on the sands of time." Anne Bradstreet puts materialism into perspective in *Upon the Burning of Our House* and Henry Vaughan exalts the wonder of the universe when he declares, with arresting immediacy, "I saw eternity the other night. . . ."

Included, too, are poems by such notable writers as George Eliot, Henry Thoreau, Robert Browning, Christina Rossetti, and John Donne. Also represented are the anonymous writers, those unknown authors each one of whom reveals unique and sensitive insights.

Henry Wadsworth Longfellow wrote that poems "have power to quiet the restless pulse of care, and come like the benediction that follows after prayer." It is hoped that these poems, like a benediction, will inspire, comfort, and bring peace to all who read and reread them.

GAIL HARVEY

NEW YORK
1990

HOPE

*H*ope is the thing with feathers
That perches in the soul,
And sings the tune without the words,
And never stops at all,

And sweetest in the gale is heard;
And sore must be the storm
That could abash the little bird
That kept so many warm.

I've heard it in the chillest land,
And on the strangest sea;
Yet, never, in extremity,
It asked a crumb of me.

EMILY DICKINSON

THE DAY IS DONE

*T*he day is done, and the darkness
   Falls from the wings of Night,
As a feather is wafted downward
   From an eagle in his flight.

I see the lights of the village
   Gleam through the rain and the mist,
And a feeling of sadness comes o'er me
   That my soul cannot resist:

A feeling of sadness and longing,
   That is not akin to pain,
And resembles sorrow only
   As the mist resembles the rain.

Come, read to me some poem,
   Some simple and heartfelt lay,
That shall soothe this restless feeling,
   And banish the thoughts of day.

Not from the grand old masters,
   Not from the bards sublime,
Whose distant footsteps echo
   Through the corridors of Time.

For like strains of martial music,
   Their mighty thoughts suggest
Life's endless toil and endeavor;
   And tonight I long for rest.

Read from some humbler poet,
   Whose songs gushed from his heart,
As showers from the clouds of summer,
   Or tears from the eyelids start;

Who, through long days of labor,
   And nights devoid of ease,
Still heard in his soul the music
   Of wonderful melodies.

Such songs have power to quiet
   The restless pulse of care,
And come like the benediction
   That follows after prayer.

Then read from the treasured volume
   The poem of thy choice,
And lend to the rhyme of the poet
   The beauty of thy voice.

And the night shall be filled with music,
   And the cares that infest the day,
Shall fold their tents like the Arabs,
   And as silently steal away.

HENRY WADSWORTH LONGFELLOW

I SHALL NOT PASS THIS WAY AGAIN

*T*hrough this toilsome world, alas!
Once and only once I pass;
If a kindness I may show,
If a good deed I may do
To a suffering fellow man,
Let me do it while I can.
No delay, for it is plain
I shall not pass this way again.

AUTHOR UNKNOWN

MAKING LIFE WORTHWHILE

*M*ay every soul that touches mine—
Be it the slightest contact—
Get therefrom some good;
Some little grace; one kindly thought;
One aspiration yet unfelt;
One bit of courage
For the darkening sky;
One gleam of faith
To brave the thickening ills of life;
One glimpse of brighter skies
Beyond the gathering mists—
To make this life worthwhile
And heaven a surer heritage.

GEORGE ELIOT

WHEN I HEARD THE LEARN'D ASTRONOMER

*W*hen I heard the learn'd astronomer,
When the proofs, the figures, were ranged in
    columns before me,
When I was shown the charts and diagrams, to add,
    divide, and measure them,
When I sitting heard the astronomer where he lectured
    with much applause in the lecture-room,
How soon unaccountable I became tired and sick,
Till rising and gliding out I wander'd off by myself,
In the mystical moist night-air, and from time to time,
Look'd up in perfect silence at the stars.

WALT WHITMAN

ON HIS BLINDNESS

*W*hen I consider how my light is spent
Ere half my days in this dark world and wide,
And that one talent, which is death to hide,
Lodged with me useless, though my soul more bent
To serve therewith my Maker, and present
My true account, lest He returning chide;
"Doth God exact day-labor, light denied?"
I fondly ask. But Patience, to prevent
That murmur, soon replies, "God doth not need
Either man's work or his own gifts; who best
Bear his mild yoke, they serve him best; his state
Is kingly; thousands at his bidding speed,
And post o'er land and ocean without rest;
They also serve who only stand and wait."

JOHN MILTON

INSPIRATION

*W*hate'er we leave to God, God does,
   And blesses us;
The work we choose should be our own,
   God lets alone.

If with light head erect I sing,
   Though all the muses lend their force,
From my poor love of anything,
   The verse is weak and shallow as its source.

But if with bended neck I grope,
   Listening behind me for my wit,
With faith superior to hope,
   More anxious to keep back than forward it.

Making my soul accomplice there
   Unto the flame my heart hath lit,
Then will the verse forever wear,—
   Time cannot bend the line which God hath writ.

Always the general show of things
   Floats in review before my mind,
And such true love and reverence brings,
   That sometimes I forget that I am blind.

But now there comes unsought, unseen,
   Some clear, divine electuary,
And I who had but sensual been,
   Grow sensible, and as God is, am wary.

I hearing get who had but ears,
  And sight, who had but eyes before,
I moments live who lived but years,
  And truth discern who knew but learning's lore.

I hear beyond the range of sound,
  I see beyond the range of sight,
New earths and skies and seas around,
  And in my day the sun doth pale his light.

A clear and ancient harmony
  Pierces my soul through all its din,
As through its utmost melody,—
  Farther behind than they—farther within.

More swift its bolt than lightning is,
  Its voice than thunder is more loud,
It doth expand my privacies
  To all, and leave me single in the crowd.

It speaks with such authority,
  With so serene and lofty tone,
That idle Time runs gadding by,
  And leaves me with Eternity alone.

Then chiefly is my natal hour,
  And only then my prime of life,
Of manhood's strength it is the flower,
  'Tis peace's end and war's beginning strife.

'T hath come in summer's broadest noon,
  By a gray wall or some chance place,
Unseasoned time, insulted June,
  And vexed the day with its presuming face.

Such fragrance round my couch it makes,
  More rich than are Arabian drugs,
That my soul scents its life and wakes
  The body up beneath its perfumed rugs.

Such is the Muse—the heavenly maid,
  The star that guides our mortal course,
Which shows where life's true kernel's laid,
  Its wheat's fine flower, and its undying force.

She with one breath attunes the spheres,
  And also my poor human heart,
With one impulse propels the years
  Around, and gives my throbbing pulse its start.

I will no doubt forever more,
  Nor falter from a steadfast faith,
For though the system be turned o'er,
  God takes not back the word which once he saith.

I will then trust the love untold
  Which not my worth nor want has bought,
Which wooed me young and woos me old,
  And to this evening hath me brought.

My memory I'll educate
  To know the one historic truth,
Remembering to the latest date
  The only true and sole immortal youth.

Be but thy inspiration given,
  No matter through what danger sought,
I'll fathom hell or climb to heaven,
  And yet esteem that cheap which love has bought.

HENRY DAVID THOREAU

} 18 {

THE COMMON PROBLEM

*T*he common problem—yours, mine, everyone's—
Is not to fancy what were fair in life
Provided it could be; but, finding first
What may be, then find how to make it fair
Up to our means—a very different thing!
My business is not to remake myself
But *make* the absolute *best* of what God made.

ROBERT BROWNING

AS I GROW OLD

*G*od keep my heart attuned to laughter
   When youth is done;
When all the days are gray days, coming after
   The warmth, the sun.
Ah! keep me then from bitterness, from grieving,
   When life seems cold;
God keep me always loving and believing
   As I grow old.

AUTHOR UNKNOWN

MIRACLES

*W*hy, who makes much of a miracle?
As to me I know of nothing else but miracles,
Whether I walk the streets of Manhattan,
Or dart my sight over the roofs of houses toward
    the sky,
Or wade with naked feet along the beach just in the
    edge of the water,
Or stand under trees in the woods,
Or talk by day with any one I love,
Or sit at table at dinner with the rest,
Or look at strangers opposite me riding in the car.
Or watch honeybees busy around the hive of a Summer
    forenoon,
Or animals feeding in the fields,
Or birds, or the wonderfulness of insects in the air,
Or the wonderfulness of the sundown, or of stars
    shining so quiet and bright,
Or the exquisite delicate thin curve of the new moon
    in Spring;
These with the rest, one and all, are to me miracles,
The whole referring, yet each distinct and in its place.

To me every hour of the light and dark is a miracle,
Every cubic inch of space is a miracle,
Every square yard of the surface of the earth is spread
    with the same,
Every foot of the interior swarms with the same.

To me the sea is a continual miracle,
The fishes that swim—the rocks—the motion of the
    waves—the ships with men in them,
What stranger miracles are there?

WALT WHITMAN

{ 21 {

CHARACTER OF A HAPPY LIFE

*H*ow happy is he born and taught
That serveth not another's will:
Whose armor is his honest thought
And simple truth his utmost skill!

Whose passions not his masters are,
Whose soul is still prepared for death,
Not tied unto the world with care
Of public fame, or private breath;

Who envies none that chance doth raise
Or vice; Who never understood
How deepest wounds are given by praise;
Nor rules of state, but rules of good;

Who hath his life from rumors freed,
Whose conscience is his strong retreat;
Whose state can neither flatterers feed,
Nor ruin make accusers great;

Who God doth late and early pray
More of His grace than gifts to lend;
And entertains the harmless day
With a well-chosen book or friend;

—This man is freed from servile bands
Of hope to rise, or fear to fall;
Lord of himself, though not of lands;
And have nothing, yet hath all.

SIR HENRY WOTTON

ABOU BEN ADHEM

*A*bou Ben Adhem—may his tribe increase—
Awoke one night from a deep dream of peace,
And saw within the moonlight in his room,
Making it rich and like a lily in bloom,
An angel writing in a book of gold.
Exceeding peace had made Ben Adhem bold,
And to the presence in the room he said:
"What writest thou?" The vision raised its head,
And with a look made all of sweet accord,
Answered: "The names of those who love the Lord."
"And is mine one?" said Abou. "Nay, not so,"
Replied the angel. Abou spoke more low,
But cheerly still; and said: "I pray thee, then,
Write me as one that loves his fellowmen."
The angel wrote, and vanished. The next night
It came again with a great wakening light,
And shewed the names whom love of God had blessed,
And lo! Ben Adhem's name led all the rest.

Leigh Hunt

A PSALM OF LIFE

*T*ell me not in mournful numbers,
  "Life is but an empty dream!"
For the soul is dead that slumbers,
  And things are not what they seem.

Life is real! Life is earnest!
  And the grave is not its goal;
"Dust thou art, to dust returnest,"
  Was not spoken of the soul.

Not enjoyment and not sorrow,
  Is our destined end or way;
But to act, that each tomorrow
  Find us farther than today.

Art is long, and time is fleeting,
  And our hearts, though stout and brave,
Still, like muffled drums are beating
  Funeral marches to the grave.

In the world's broad field of battle,
  In the bivouac of life,
Be not like dumb, driven cattle!
  Be a hero in the strife!

Trust no future, howe'er pleasant!
  Let the dead past bury its dead!
Act, act in the living present!
  Heart within and God o'erhead!

Lives of great men all remind us
  We can make our lives sublime,
And, departing, leave behind us
  Footprints on the sands of time.

Footprints, that perhaps another,
  Sailing o'er life's solemn main,
A forlorn and shipwrecked brother,
  Seeing, shall take heart again.

Let us, then, be up and doing,
  With a heart for any fate;
Still achieving, still pursuing,
  Learn to labor and to wait.

HENRY WADSWORTH LONGFELLOW

BALLAD OF THE TEMPEST

*W*e were crowded in the cabin,
　Not a soul would dare to sleep,—
It was midnight on the waters,
　And a storm was on the deep.

'Tis a fearful thing in winter
　To be shattered by the blast,
And to hear the rattling trumpet
　Thunder, "Cut away the mast!"

So we shuddered there in silence,—
　For the stoutest held his breath,
While the hungry sea was roaring
　And the breakers talked with death.

As thus we sat in darkness
　Each one busy with his prayers,
"We are lost!" the captain shouted,
　As he staggered down the stairs.

But his little daughter whispered,
　As she took his icy hand,
"Isn't God upon the ocean,
　Just the same as on the land?"

Then we kissed the little maiden,
　And we spake in better cheer,
And we anchored safe in harbor
　When the morn was shining clear.

JAMES T. FIELDS

LIFE'S LESSONS

I learn, as the years roll onward
    And leave the past behind,
That much I had counted sorrow
    But proves that God is kind;
That many a flower I had longed for
    Had hidden a thorn of pain,
And many a rugged bypath
    Led to fields of ripened grain.

The clouds that cover the sunshine
    They cannot banish the sun;
And the earth shines out the brighter
    When the weary rain is done.
We must stand in the deepest shadow
    To see the clearest light;
And often through wrong's own darkness
    Comes the very strength of light.

The sweetest rest is at even,
    After a wearisome day,
When the heavy burden of labor
    Has borne from our hearts away;
And those who have never known sorrow
    Can not know the infinite peace
That falls on the troubled spirit
    When it sees at least release.

We must live through the dreary winter
    If we would value the spring;
And the woods must be cold and silent
    Before the robins sing.
The flowers must be buried in darkness
    Before they can bud and bloom,
And the sweetest, warmest sunshine
    Comes after the storm and gloom.

AUTHOR UNKNOWN

UPON THE BURNING OF OUR HOUSE

*I*n silent night when rest I took,
For sorrow near I did not look,
I waken'd was with thundring noise
And piteous shrieks of dreadful voice.
That fearful sound of "Fire!" and "Fire!"
Let no man know is my Desire.

I, starting up, the light did spy,
And to my God my heart did cry
To strengthen me in my Distress,
And not to leave me succourless.
Then coming out, beheld apace
The flame consume my dwelling place.

And when I could no longer look,
I blest his Name that gave and took,
That laid my goods now in the dust:
Yea so it was, and so 'twas just.
It was his own: it was not mine;
Far be it that I should repine.

He might of All justly bereft,
But yet sufficient for us left.
When by the Ruins oft I past,
My sorrowing eyes aside did cast,
And here and there the places spy
Where oft I sat, and long did lie.

Here stood that Trunk, and there that chest;
There lay that store I counted best:
My pleasant things in ashes lie,
And them behold no more shall I.
Under thy roof no guest shall sit,
Nor at thy Table eat a bit.

No pleasant tale shall e'er be told,
Nor things recounted done of old.
No Candle e'er shall shine in Thee,
Nor bridegroom's voice e'er heard shall be.
In silence ever shalt thou lie;
Adeiu, Adeiu; All's vanity.

Then straight I 'gan my heart to chide:
And did thy wealth on earth abide?
Didst fix thy hope on moldring dust,
The arm of flesh didst make thy trust?
Raise up thy thoughts above the sky,
That dunghill mists away may fly.

Thou hast a house on high erect,
Fram'd by that mighty Architect,
With glory richly furnished,
Stands permanent though this be fled.
It's purchased, and paid for, too,
By Him who hath enough to do.

A Prize so vast as is unknown,
Yet, by his Gift, is made thine own.
There's wealth enough, I need no more;
Farewell my Pelf, farewell my Store.
The world no longer let me Love,
My Hope and Treasure lies Above.

ANNE BRADSTREET

THE LOOM OF TIME

*M*an's life is laid in the loom of time
  To a pattern he does not see,
While the weavers work and the shuttles fly
  Till the dawn of eternity.

Some shuttles are filled with silver threads
  And some with threads of gold,
While often but the darker hues
  Are all that they may hold.

But the weaver watches with skillful eye
  Each shuttle fly to and fro,
And sees the pattern so deftly wrought
  As the loom moves sure and slow.

God surely planned the pattern:
  Each thread, the dark and fair,
Is chosen by His master skill
  And placed in the web with care.

He only knows its beauty,
  And guides the shuttles which hold
The threads so unattractive,
  As well as the threads of gold.

Not till each loom is silent,
  And the shuttles cease to fly,
Shall God reveal the pattern
  And explain the reason why

The dark threads were as needful
  In the weaver's skillful hand
As the threads of gold and silver
  For the pattern which He planned.

AUTHOR UNKNOWN

WHATEVER IS—IS BEST

I know, as my life grows older,
　And mine eyes have clearer sight,
That under each rank wrong somewhere
　There lies the root of Right;

That each sorrow has its purpose,
　By the sorrowing oft unguessed;
But as sure as the sun brings morning,
　Whatever is—is best.

I know that each sinful action,
　As sure as the night brings shade,
Is somewhere, sometime punished,
　Tho' the hour be long delayed.
I know that the soul is aided
　Sometimes by the heart's unrest,
And to grow means often to suffer—
　But whatever is—is best.

I know there are no errors,
　In the great Eternal plan,
And all things work together
　For the final good of man.
And I know when my soul speeds onward,
　In its grand Eternal quest,
I shall say as I look back earthward,
　Whatever is—is best.

ELLA WHEELER WILCOX

THE OLD MAN DREAMS

O for one hour of youthful joy!
　　Give back my twentieth spring!
I'd rather laugh, a bright-haired boy,
　　Than reign, a gray-beard king.

Off with the spoils of wrinkled age!
　　Away with Learning's crown!
Tear out life's Wisdom-written page,
　　And dash its trophies down!

One moment let my life-blood stream
　　From boyhood's fount of flame!
Give me one giddy, reeling dream
　　Of life all love and fame!

My listening angel heard the prayer,
　　And, calmly smiling, said,
"If I but touch thy silvered hair
　　Thy hasty wish hath sped.

"But is there nothing in thy track,
　　To bid thee fondly stay,
While the swift seasons hurry back
　　To find the wished-for day?"

"Ah, truest soul of womankind!
　　Without thee what were life?
One bliss I cannot leave behind:
　　I'll take—my—precious—wife!"

—The angel took a sapphire pen
   And wrote in rainbow dew,
The man would be a boy again,
   And be a husband too!

"And is there nothing yet unsaid,
   Before the change appears?
Remember, all their gifts have fled
   With those dissolving years."

"Why yes"; for memory would recall
   My fond paternal joys;
"I could not bear to leave them all—
   I'll take—my—girl—and—boys."

The smiling angel dropped his pen,—
   "Why this will never do;
The man would be a boy again,
   And be a father too!"

And so I laughed,—my laughter woke
   The household with its noise,—
And wrote my dream, when morning broke,
   To please the gray-haired boys.

OLIVER WENDELL HOLMES

JUNE

*A*nd what is so rare as a day in June?
  Then, if ever, come perfect days;
Then heaven tries the earth if it be in tune,
  And over it softly her warm ear lays;
Whether we look, or whether we listen,
We hear life murmur, or see it glisten;
Every clod feels a stir of might.
  An instinct within it that reaches and towers,
And, groping blindly above it for light,
  Climbs to a soul in grasses and flowers;
The flush of life may well be seen
  Thrilling back over hills and valleys;
The cowslip startles in meadows green,
  The buttercup catches the sun in its chalice,
And there's never a leaf nor a blade too mean
  To be some happy creature's palace;
The little bird sits at his door in the sun,
  Atilt like a blossom among the leaves,
And lets his illumined being o'errun
  With the deluge of summer it receives;
His mate feels the eggs beneath her wings,
And the heart in her dumb breast flutters and sings;
He sings to the wide world, and she to her nest—
In the nice ear of nature, which song is the best?

JAMES RUSSELL LOWELL

THE FOOL'S PRAYER

*T*he royal feast was done; the King
  Sought some new sport to banish care,
And to his jester cried: "Sir Fool,
  Kneel now, and make for us a prayer!"

The jester doffed his cap and bells,
  And stood the mocking court before;
They could not see the bitter smile
  Behind the painted grin he wore.

He bowed his head, and bent his knee
  Upon the monarch's silken stool;
His pleading voice arose: "O Lord,
  Be merciful to me, a fool!

"No pity, Lord, could change the heart
  From red with wrong to white as wool;
The rod must heal the sin: but Lord,
  Be merciful to me, a fool!

" 'Tis not by guilt the onward sweep
  Of truth and right, O Lord, we stay;
'Tis by our follies that so long
  We hold the earth from heaven away.

"These clumsy feet, still in the mire,
  Go crushing blossoms without end;
These hard, well-meaning hands we thrust
  Among the heartstrings of a friend.

"The ill-timed truth we might have kept—
   Who knows how sharp it pierced and stung?
The word we had not sense to say—
   Who knows how grandly it had rung!

"Our faults no tenderness should ask,
   The chastening stripes must cleanse them all;
But for our blunders—oh, in shame
   Before the eyes of heaven we fall.

"Earth bears no balsam for mistakes;
   Men crown the knave, and scourge the tool
That did his will; but Thou, O Lord,
   Be merciful to me, a fool!"

The room was hushed; in silence rose
   The King, and sought his gardens cool,
And walked apart, and murmured low,
   "Be merciful to me, a fool!"

EDWARD ROWLAND SILL

THE BUILDERS

*A*ll are architects of Fate,
   Working in these walls of Time;
Some with massive deeds and great,
   Some with ornaments of rhyme.

Nothing useless is, or low;
   Each thing in its place is best;
And what seems but idle show
   Strengthens and supports the rest.

For the structure that we raise,
   Time is with materials filled;
Our todays and yesterdays
   Are the blocks with which we build.

Truly shape and fashion these;
   Leave no yawning gaps between;
Think not, because no man sees,
   Such things will remain unseen.

In the elder days of Art,
   Builders wrought with greatest care
Each minute and unseen part;
   For the Gods see everywhere.

Let us do our work as well,
   Both the unseen and the seen!
Make the house, where Gods may dwell,
   Beautiful, entire, and clean.

Else our lives are incomplete,
    Standing in these walls of Time,
Broken stairways, where the feet
    Stumble as they seek to climb.

Build today, then, strong and sure,
    With a firm and ample base;
And ascending and secure
    Shall tomorrow find its place.

Thus alone can we attain
    To those turrets, where the eye
Sees the world as one vast plain,
    And one boundless reach of sky.

HENRY WADSWORTH LONGFELLOW

SONNET

To one who has been long in city pent,
  'Tis very sweet to look into the fair
  And open face of heaven,—to breathe a prayer
Full in the smile of the blue firmament.
Who is more happy, when, with heart content,
  Fatigued he sinks into some pleasant lair
  Of wavy grass, and reads a debonair
And gentle tale of love and languishment?
  Returning home at evening, with an ear
Catching the notes of Philomel,—an eye
  Watching the sailing cloudlet's bright career,
He mourns that day so soon has glided by:
  E'en like the passage of an angel's tear
That falls through the clear ether silently.

JOHN KEATS

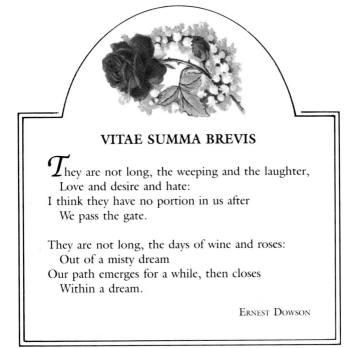

VITAE SUMMA BREVIS

*T*hey are not long, the weeping and the laughter,
  Love and desire and hate:
I think they have no portion in us after
  We pass the gate.

They are not long, the days of wine and roses:
  Out of a misty dream
Our path emerges for a while, then closes
  Within a dream.

Ernest Dowson

AFTER THE STORM

*T*he seas are quiet when the winds give o'er;
So calm are we when passions are no more:
For then we know how vain it was to boast
Of fleeting things, so certain to be lost:
Clouds of affection from our younger eyes
Conceal that emptiness which age descries.

The soul's dark cottage, battered and decayed,
Lets in new light through chinks that time has made
Stronger by weakness: wiser men become,
As they draw near to their eternal home:
Leaving the Old, both Worlds at once they view,
That stand upon the threshold of the New.

EDMUND WALLER

THANATOPSIS

To him who in the love of Nature holds
Communion with her visible forms, she speaks
A various language; for his gayer hours
She has a voice of gladness, and a smile
And eloquence of beauty, and she glides
Into his darker musings, with a mild
And healing sympathy, that steals away
Their sharpness, ere he is aware. When thoughts
Of the last bitter hour come like a blight
Over thy spirit, and sad images
Of the stern agony, and shroud, and pall,
And breathless darkness, and the narrow house,
Make thee to shudder, and grow sick at heart;—
Go forth, under the open sky, and list
To Nature's teachings, while from all around—
Earth and her waters, and the depths of air—
Comes a still voice— Yet a few days, and thee
The all-beholding sun shall see no more
In all his course; nor yet in the cold ground,
Where thy pale form was laid, with many tears,
Nor in the embrace of ocean, shall exist
Thy image. Earth, that nourished thee, shall claim
Thy growth, to be resolved to earth again,
And, lost each human trace, surrendering up
Thine individual being, shalt thou go
To mix for ever with the elements,
To be a brother to the insensible rock
And to the sluggish clod, which the rude swain
Turns with his share, and treads upon. The oak
Shall send his roots abroad, and pierce thy mould.

Yet not to thine eternal resting-place
Shalt thou retire alone, nor couldst thou wish
Couch more magnificent. Thou shalt lie down
With patriarchs of the infant world—with kings,
The powerful of the earth—the wise, the good,
Fair forms, and hoary seers of ages past,
All in one mighty sepulchre. The hills
Rock-ribbed and ancient as the sun,—the vales
Stretching in pensive quietness between;
The venerable woods—rivers that move
In majesty, and the complaining brooks
That make the meadows green; and, poured round all,
Old Ocean's gray and melancholy waste,—
Are but the solemn decorations all
Of the great tomb of man. The golden sun,
The planets, all the infinite host of heaven,
Are shining on the sad abodes of death,
Through the still lapse of ages. All that tread
The globe are but a handful to the tribes
That slumber in its bosom. —Take the wings
Of morning, pierce the Barcan wilderness,
Or lose thyself in the continuous woods
Where rolls the Oregon, and hears no sound,
Save his own dashings—yet the dead are there:
And millions in those solitudes, since first
The flight of years began, have laid them down
In their last sleep—the dead reign there alone.

So shalt thou rest, and what if thou withdraw
In silence from the living, and no friend
Take note of thy departure? All that breathe
Will share thy destiny. The gay will laugh
When thou art gone, the solemn brood of care
Plod on, and each one as before will chase
His favorite phantom; yet all these shall leave
Their mirth and their employments, and shall come
And make their bed with thee. As the long train
Of ages glide away, the sons of men,
The youth in life's green spring, and he who goes
In the full strength of years, matron and maid,
The speechless babe, and the gray-headed man—
Shall one by one be gathered to thy side,
By those, who in their turn shall follow them.

   So live, that when thy summons comes to join
The innumerable caravan, which moves
To that mysterious realm, where each shall take
His chamber in the silent halls of death,
Thou go not, like the quarry-slave at night,
Scourged to his dungeon, but, sustained and soothed
By an unfaltering trust, approach thy grave,
Like one who wraps the drapery of his couch
About him, and lies down to pleasant dreams.

WILLIAM CULLEN BRYANT

THE SIGNATURE OF GOD

*H*appy choristers of air,
Who by your nimble flight draw near
   His throne, whose wondrous story,
   And unconfinëd glory
Your notes still carol, whom your sound
And whom your plumy pipes rebound.

Yet do the lazy snails no less
The greatness of our Lord confess,
   And those whom weight hath chained
   And to the earth restrained,
Their ruder voices do as well,
Yea, and the speechless fishes tell.

Great Lord, from whom each tree receives,
Then pays again, as rent, his leaves;
   Thou dost in purple set
   The rose and violet,
And giv'st the sickly lily white;
Yet in them all thy name dost write.

JOHN HALL

FLOWERS OF NIGHT

*C*hildren of night! unfolding meekly, slowly
To the sweet breathings of the shadowy hours,
When dark blue heavens look softest and most holy,
And glow-worm light is in the forest bowers;
    To solemn things and deep,
    To spirit-haunted sleep,
    To thoughts, all purified
    From earth, ye seem allied;
        O dedicated flowers!

Ye, from the gaze of crowds your beauty veiling,
Keep in dim vestal urns the sweetness shrined;
Till the mild moon, on high serenely sailing,
Looks on you tenderly and sadly kind.
    So doth love's dreaming heart
    Dwell from the throng apart,
    And but to shades disclose
    The inmost thought which glows
        With its pure heart entwined.

Shut from the sounds wherein the day rejoices,
To no triumphant song your petals thrill,
But send forth odors with the faint, soft voices
Rising from hidden streams, when all is still.
    So doth lone prayer arise,
    Mingling with secret sighs,
    When grief unfolds, like you,
    Her breast, for heavenly dew
        In silent hours to fill.

FELICIA HEMANS

GOD MOVES IN A MYSTERIOUS WAY

God moves in a mysterious way
   His wonders to perform;
He plants his footsteps in the sea,
   And rides upon the storm.

Deep in unfathomable mines,
   With never-failing skill,
He treasures up his bright designs,
   And works his sovereign will.

Judge not the Lord by feeble sense,
   But trust him for his grace;
Behind a frowning providence
   He hides a smiling face.

His purposes will ripen fast,
   Unfolding every hour;
The bud may have a bitter taste,
   But sweet will be the flower.

Blind unbelief is sure to err,
   And scan his work in vain;
God is his own interpreter,
   And he will make it plain.

Ye fearful saints fresh courage take,
   The clouds you so much dread
Are big with mercy and shall break,
   With blessings on your head.

WILLIAM COWPER

SWEET DAY

Sweet day, so cool, so calm, so bright!
  The bridal of the earth and sky—
The dew shall weep thy fall tonight;
  For thou must die.

Sweet rose, whose hue angry and brave
  Bids the rash gazer wipe his eye,
Thy root is ever in its grave,
  And thou must die.

Sweet spring, full of sweet days and roses,
  A box where sweets compacted lie,
My music shows ye have your closes,
  And all must die.

Only a sweet and virtuous soul,
  Like seasoned timber, never gives;
But though the whole world turn to coal,
  Then chiefly lives.

GEORGE HERBERT

NOT AS I WILL

*B*lindfolded and alone I stand,
With unknown thresholds on each hand;
The darkness deepens as I grope,
Afraid to fear, afraid to hope;
Yet this one thing I learn to know
Each day more surely as I go,
That doors are opened, ways are made,
Burdens are lifted or are laid
By some great law, unseen and still,
Unfathomed purpose to fulfil,
   "Not as I will."

Blindfolded and alone I wait;
Loss seems too bitter, gain too late;
Too heavy burdens in the load
And too few helpers on the road,
And joy is weak and grief is strong,
And years and days so long, so long;
Yet this one thing I learn to know
Each day more surely as I go,
That I am glad the good and ill
By changeless law are ordered still,
   "Not as I will."

"Not as I will"; the sound grows sweet
Each time my lips the words repeat,
"Not as I will"; the darkness feels
More safe than light when this thought steals
Like whispered voice to calm and bless
All unrest and all loneliness.
"Not as I will," because the One
Who loves us first and best has gone
Before us on the road, and still
For us must all His love fulfil,
   "Not as we will."

THE DEATH OF THE FLOWERS

*T*he melancholy days are come, the saddest of the year,
Of wailing winds, and naked woods, and meadows brown
    and sere.
Heaped in the hollows of the grove, the autumn leaves lie dead;
They rustle to the eddying gust, and to the rabbit's tread;
The robin and the wren are flown, and from the shrubs the jay,
And from the wood-top calls the crow through all the
    gloomy day.

Where are the flowers, the fair young flowers, that lately
    sprang and stood
In brighter light and softer airs, a beauteous sisterhood?
Alas! they all are in their graves, the gentle race of flowers
Are lying in their lowly beds, with the fair and good of ours.
The rain is falling where they lie, but the cold November rain
Calls not from out the gloomy earth the lovely ones again.

The windflower and the violet, they perished long ago,
And the brier rose and the orchis died amid the summer glow;
But on the hills the goldenrod, and the aster in the wood,
And the yellow sunflower by the brook in autumn beauty
    stood,
Till fell the frost from the clear cold heaven, as fall as plague
    on men,
And the brightness of their smile was gone, from upland, glade,
    and glen.

And now, when comes the calm mild day, as still such days
    will come,
To call the squirrel and the bee from out their winter home;
When the sound of dropping nuts is heard, though all the trees
    are still,
And twinkle in the smoky light the waters of the rill,
The south wind searches for the flowers whose fragrance late
    he bore,
And sighs to find them in the wood and by the stream no more.

And then I think of one who in her youthful beauty died,
The fair meek blossom that grew up and faded by my side.
In the cold moist earth we laid her, when the forests cast
    the leaf,
And we wept that one so lovely should have a life so brief:
Yet not unmeet it was that one, like that young friend of ours,
So gentle and so beautiful, should perish with the flowers.

WILLIAM CULLEN BRYANT

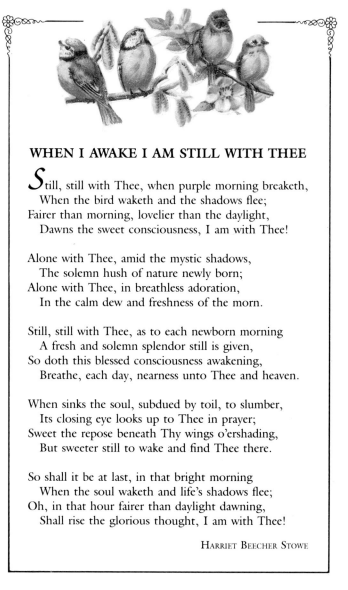

WHEN I AWAKE I AM STILL WITH THEE

*S*till, still with Thee, when purple morning breaketh,
 When the bird waketh and the shadows flee;
Fairer than morning, lovelier than the daylight,
 Dawns the sweet consciousness, I am with Thee!

Alone with Thee, amid the mystic shadows,
 The solemn hush of nature newly born;
Alone with Thee, in breathless adoration,
 In the calm dew and freshness of the morn.

Still, still with Thee, as to each newborn morning
 A fresh and solemn splendor still is given,
So doth this blessed consciousness awakening,
 Breathe, each day, nearness unto Thee and heaven.

When sinks the soul, subdued by toil, to slumber,
 Its closing eye looks up to Thee in prayer;
Sweet the repose beneath Thy wings o'ershading,
 But sweeter still to wake and find Thee there.

So shall it be at last, in that bright morning
 When the soul waketh and life's shadows flee;
Oh, in that hour fairer than daylight dawning,
 Shall rise the glorious thought, I am with Thee!

HARRIET BEECHER STOWE

IT IS A BEAUTEOUS EVENING

*I*t is a beauteous evening, calm and free,
The holy time is quiet as a Nun
Breathless with adoration; the broad sun
Is sinking down in its tranquillity;
The gentleness of heaven broods o'er the Sea:
Listen! the mighty Being is awake,
And doth with his eternal motion make
A sound like thunder—everlastingly.
Dear Child! dear Girl! that walkest with me here,
If thou appear untouched by solemn thought,
Thy nature is not therefore less divine:
Thou liest in Abraham's bosom all the year;
And worshipp'st at the Temple's inner shrine,
God being with thee when we know it not.

WILLIAM WORDSWORTH

REMEMBER

*R*emember me when I am gone away,
Gone far away into the silent land;
When you can no more hold me by the hand,
Nor I half turn to go, yet turning stay.
Remember me when no more, day by day,
You tell me of our future that you planned:
Only remember me; you understand
It will be late to counsel then or pray.
Yet if you should forget me for a while
And afterwards remember, do not grieve:
For if the darkness and corruption leave
A vestige of the thoughts that once I had,
Better by far you should forget and smile
Than that you should remember and be sad.

CHRISTINA ROSSETTI

HEAVEN LIES ABOUT US

*Y*e blessed creatures, I have heard the call
  Ye to each other make; I see
The heavens laugh with you in your jubilee;
  My heart is at your festival,
  My head hath its coronal,
The fulness of your bliss, I feel—I feel it all.
  Oh evil day! if I were sullen
  While Earth herself is adorning,
   This sweet May morning,
  And the children are culling,
   On every side,
  In a thousand valleys far and wide,
  Fresh flowers; while the sun shines warm,
And the babe leaps up on his mother's arm:—
  I hear, I hear, with joy I hear!
  —But there's a tree, of many, one,
A single field which I have looked upon,
Both of them speak of something that is gone:
  The pansy at my feet
  Doth the same tale repeat:
Whither is fled the visionary gleam?
Where is it now, the glory and the dream?

Our birth is but a sleep and a forgetting:
The soul that rises with us, our life's star,
Hath had elsewhere its setting,
And cometh from afar:
Not in entire forgetfulness,
And not in utter nakedness,
But trailing clouds of glory do we come,
From God, who is our home:
Heaven lies about us in our infancy!
Shades of the prison-house begin to close
Upon the growing boy,
But he beholds the light, and whence it flows,
He sees it in his joy;
The youth, who daily farther from the east
Must travel, still is Nature's Priest,
And by the vision splendid
Is on his way attended;
At length the man perceives it die away,
And fade into the light of common day.

WILLIAM WORDSWORTH

THE PASSING DAY

A late lark twitters from the quiet skies;
And from the west,
Where the sun, his day's work ended,
Lingers as in content,
There falls on the old, gray city
An influence luminous and serene
A shining peace.

The smoke ascends
In a rosy and golden haze. The spires
Shine, and are changed. In the valley
Shadows rise. The lark sings on. The sun,
Closing his benediction,
Sinks, and the darkening air
Thrills with a sense of the triumphing night—
Night, with her train of stars
And her great gift of sleep.

So be my passing!
My task accomplished and the long day done,
My wages taken, and in my heart
Some late lark singing,
Let me be gathered to the quiet west,
The sundown splendid and serene,
Death.

WILLIAM ERNEST HENLEY

THE LORD IS MY SHEPHERD

*T*he Lord is my shepherd; I shall not want.
He maketh me to lie down in green pastures:
  he leadeth me beside the still waters.
He restoreth my soul: he leadeth me in the
  paths of righteousness for his name's sake.
Yea, though I walk through the valley of the
  shadow of death, I will fear no evil:
    for thou art with me;
    thy rod and thy staff they comfort me.
Thou preparest a table before me in the
  presence of mine enemies:
    thou anointest my head with oil;
    my cup runneth over.
Surely goodness and mercy shall follow me
  all the days of my life: and I will dwell
  in the house of the Lord forever.

Psalm 23

CHARTLESS

I never saw a moor,
 I never saw the sea,
Yet know I how the heather looks,
 And what a wave must be.

I never spoke with God,
 Nor visited in heaven;
Yet certain am I of the spot
 As if the chart were given.

EMILY DICKINSON

THE SOUL'S GARMENT

*G*reat Nature clothes the soul, which is but thin,
With fleshly garments, which the Fates do spin;
And when these garments are grown old and bare,
With sickness torn, Death takes them off with care,
And folds them up in peace and quiet rest,
And lays them safe within an earthly chest:
Then scours them well and makes them sweet and clean,
Fit for the soul to wear those clothes again.

MARGARET CAVENDISH, DUCHESS OF NEWCASTLE

DEATH, BE NOT PROUD

*D*eath, be not proud, though some have called thee
Mighty and dreadful, for thou art not so;
For those whom thou think'st thou dost overthrow
Die not, poor Death, nor yet canst thou kill me.
From rest and sleep, which but thy pictures be,
Much pleasure; then from thee much more must flow,
And soonest our best men with thee do go,
Rest of their bones, and soul's delivery.
Thou art slave to fate, chance, kings, and desperate men,
And dost with poison, war, and sickness dwell;
And poppy or charms can make us sleep as well
And better than thy stroke; why swell'st thou then?
One short sleep past, we wake eternally,
And death shall be no more; Death, thou shalt die.

JOHN DONNE

THE MOTION OF THE SPHERES

I saw eternity the other night
Like a great ring of pure and endless light,
   All calm, as it was bright;
And, round beneath it, time, in hours, days, years,
   Driven by the spheres,
Like a vast shadow moved, in which the world
   And all her train were hurled.

HENRY VAUGHAN